BETTER BUSINESS

A *QUICK* (

WRITING
BETTER EMAILS

HEATHER WRIGHT

Heather Wright
hwrightwriter@gmail.com

Better Business Communication
A Quick Guide to Writing Better Emails / Heather Wright. —1st ed.
ISBN 9781517556525

Get the entire Better Business Communication series in **ONE, COST-SAVING VOLUME**! The complete contents of

- *A Quick Guide to Writing Better Email*
- *A Quick Guide to Better Writing & Grammar*
- *A Quick Guide to Better Presentations,* and
- *A Quick Guide to Better Telephone Skills* are all **here**:

Check your online bookstore for more details

Contents

Introduction

This book is **your quick guide to writing better emails**. Ten short chapters outline the strategies you need for writing emails that get the responses you want and mark you as a professional.

People spend a lot of time on their computers or smartphones communicating for fun. Facebook, Twitter, and instant messaging have made us very fond of short forms, acronyms and multiple punctuation marks!!! But business writing is different.

Writing for business has two purposes:

1. **to make your company look good.**
2. **to make you look good.**

In ancient times, such as those when I first went to work in an office, managers had secretaries. Managers dictated letters and secretaries typed them up, corrected the grammar, and were responsible for accurate spelling and formatting.

Those days are gone. There is no skilled buffer between your thoughts and the words that go to your clients, co-workers, and your boss.

And the pace has changed, too. Letters could be proofread, retyped, and changed again, before they were finally put in the mailbox at the end of the day.

The recipient knew that it could take a week before he or she got the answer to the original letter.

Business today would collapse with that kind of time line. The expectation is that email gets answered within a matter of hours or even parts of hours. **Quick response is expected**.

Your limited time is the reason that this book is short. You don't have the time to muddle through a large text. You need quick fixes fast. Read this book from the beginning or just read the chapters that apply to the questions you have now.

Other books currently being released in this Better Business Communication series cover the topics of presentations, writing and grammar, and telephone skills and are available at your online bookstore.

CHAPTER 1

Making the Subject Line Do Its Job

The subject line gets your email opened, so it needs to do its job. Subject lines need to be clear and also have enough information in them to help the recipient prioritize his or her response.

Let's face it; email boxes fill up quickly. If you want an answer to your email, you have to let your reader know your email's purpose right away. No cute half sentences to make the reader open the email to read the rest. No silly references to sex or money to trick the reader into opening the mail. No "You won't want to miss this!!!"

Your email subject line should be an effective summary of the email's contents with enough information for the reader to decide if it's urgent or not. And please don't bother to mark your email *urgent*. If an issue really is urgent, pick up the phone. Half of your reader's correspondents think their emails are urgent, too. After a while, it gets to be very easy to ignore those red exclamation marks.

Let's have a look at some examples.

Example 1

You are asking your co-workers to complete a short survey to help HR choose next year's benefits package. Here are some options that will get your request ignored and one that will likely work:

Re: HR Survey
Reader response: Another one? Don't have time for this.

Re: Benefits
Reader response: I'll look at that later.

Re: Benefits Survey
Reader response: I'll look at that later.

Re: Short Survey for Your 2016 Benefits' Package Due April 4th
Reader response: I'd better do that now before I forget. This subject line works for a couple of reasons. 1) Using the word "your" takes the topic away from the impersonal. Completing the survey will directly affect the reader. 2) A date is mentioned. The reader is more likely to respond if he or she knows that the time for input is limited. 3) The word "short" is encouraging.

The reader feels he or she can take the time to do it now, without losing too much valuable time.

Example 2

You've discovered an excellent online course on warehouse management that you want to take. A couple of your co-workers have already taken it and found it very valuable. You have to write to the boss to ask for funding for the course. Here are some options that will get your request ignored and one that will likely work:

Re: Online Course
Reader response: Haven't a clue what that's about. I'll leave it until later.

Re: Request for Online Course
Reader response: Does he/she want to take one of the company courses? Someone else's? I'll leave it until later.

Re: Requesting Funding for Warehouse Management Online Course
Reader response: I remember that course. Bill and Maria took it. Very valuable. Let's get this cleared away now.

IN SHORT

Email subject lines should

- Use capital letters on all words except short prepositions and conjunctions. (See samples above.)
- Give the reader enough information to be able to decide how to prioritize his or her response.
- Include a date if the response has to be timely.
- Avoid jokes, lots of punctuation, and vague statements or teasers.

The Salutation—Saying Hello

Email resembles letters in many ways, but since so few people write letters, it's worthwhile to remind you about salutations.

Always begin your email message with a greeting. Here are some examples:

- *Hi,* or *Hi Harriet,*
- *Dear Harriet,* - use the recipient's first name, if you know the person, or if that's the way they signed their email to you.
- *Dear Mr. Wilson,* - use a more formal approach, if the person is a stranger or if you are aware that the person has influence in your company. When you are writing to senior management, especially if the person is older, a more formal approach is usually more appropriate.
- Never write Dear Mr. Jim Wilson. The correct salutations are either Dear Jim or Dear Mr. Wilson.
- Another method is to use the person's name in the first sentence, for example: *Thanks,*

Bill, for getting back to me so quickly. Use commas on either side of the person's name to punctuate your sentence correctly.

IN SHORT

- Always use a salutation or include the recipient's name in the first sentence.
- Hi, Dear First Name, or Dear Surname are your best choices followed by a comma.

CHAPTER 3

Begin with the Purpose

If you are writing an email that is delivering information, or asking a question, or thanking someone, there's no need to keep the purpose a secret. Putting the purpose of your email in the first paragraph is just fine.

If you know that the person has been away sick or is coming back from vacation, it's okay to make a one line reference to that, as well.

Here are a couple of examples.

Example 1

Dear Leslie,

Welcome back from holidays. I hope you had a great time in Florida.

While you were away, several changes were made to the Benson contract. Here's a summary of the changes that we will be discussing at Friday's meeting … *and the rest of the email lists the changes to the contract.*

Example 2

Thanks for getting back to me so quickly, Micah. I've thought of one more question since we last spoke. Which date did the client agree upon for the final payment?

In the first example, the email could have started fine without the reference to the holidays. In the second example, the information needed is referred to in the first paragraph.

IN SHORT

Without being too abrupt or curt, get to the point of your email early. With so many emails landing in people's mailboxes these days, readers have a tendency to skim in an effort to move through their mailbox quickly. Get your information up front before your reader's attention wanders.

CHAPTER 4

Building the Message

Email is broken into short paragraphs for a couple of reasons. 1) A new paragraph is required for a new topic. 2) Short paragraphs separated by empty lines look a lot more reader-friendly and inviting on the screen than a dense block of text.

A Note about Grammar and Spelling

The sentences in your paragraphs should be complete. They should begin with a capital letter and end with a period. Your spelling should be correct. The purpose of correct grammar and spelling is to make your writing look professional and for your message to be as accessible and easy-to-read as possible. If a client or your boss has to reread a sentence a couple of times to figure out what you are saying, the response to your email might just reflect his or her frustration.

Correct punctuation and use of capitals tells your reader that you care about the quality of your work. It may seem like a small thing, but **it builds trust**. Imagine if you are a financial planner writing to your client. If you don't take the time to make sure that the spelling and grammar of your message are correct, why should the client trust that you would take care of the details in his or her financial plan?

The Middle of the Message

After you have explained the purpose of the email, the middle paragraph or paragraphs are used to add more details that your reader might need in order to make a decision. **Use a new paragraph for each new topic**. If you have several points to cover or pieces of information to deliver, consider using a bulleted list. The **Rules for Bulleted Lists are in Chapter 6**.

If you are responding to a list of questions or concerns, **copy the list of questions or concerns from the original email into your reply**, and answer each one, typing your answer below the question. If you do this, you will ensure that you have answered all the questions or addressed all the concerns that were sent in the original email. Preface your list with the words *Here are the answers to the questions you sent on Tuesday.*

Here's how the letter begun in step 3 might continue:

Dear Leslie,

Welcome back from holidays. I hope you had a great time in Florida.

While you were away, several changes were made to the Benson contract. Here's a summary of the changes that we will be discussing at Friday's meeting:

1. Paragraph 4 – Parker Co. is changed to Parker Company. This change is continued throughout the contract.
2. Paragraph 12 – The sum of restitution has been changed to $20,000 from $10,000.
3. Paragraphs 20 to 30 – Note the changes here to the partnership agreement requested by Helen.
4. Paragraph 42 – Note the change to insurance coverage that has been requested by Helen.

IN SHORT

- Use short paragraphs.
- Each paragraph should deal with a new topic.
- Make sure that spelling and grammar are correct.
- Copy questions from the original email into your reply and answer each one.

CHAPTER 5

Writing the Ending

The last paragraph of an email is the place where you insert the call to action (if necessary), wrap up your message, and say thanks or that you are looking forward to hearing from the recipient again.

The end of an email includes a complimentary close. These tend to be short and include the following:

Best regards,

Regards,

Yours truly,

Sincerely,

The complimentary close should be followed by your first name and your email signature that includes your full name, your position with the company, your email address, and your phone number. You can set these up on your email program to be added automatically to all of your correspondence. The end of the message begun in Step 3 might look like this:

Dear Leslie,

Welcome back from holidays. I hope you had a great time in Florida.

While you were away, several changes were made to the Benson contract. Here's a summary of the changes that we will be discussing at Friday's meeting:

1. Paragraph 4 – Parker Co. is changed to Parker Company. This change is continued throughout the contract.
2. Paragraph 12 – The sum of restitution has been changed to $20,000 from $10,000.
3. Paragraphs 20 to 30 – Note the changes here to the partnership agreement requested by Helen.
4. Paragraph 42 – Note the change to insurance coverage that has been requested by Helen.

I look forward to seeing you on Friday and hearing your views on the above changes. If you have any questions in the meantime, please give me a call at ext. 32.

Best regards,

Heather

Heather Wright
Vice-President
555-123-4567 ext. 89

hwright@thecompany.com

IN SHORT

- Include a complimentary close.
- Set up an email signature to include all necessary contact info.
- Include a call to action in the final paragraph and mention how you can be contacted.

CHAPTER 6

Cutting the Fat

Here are some tricks for cutting the fat in your email correspondence. In order to sound formal and serious, writers often resort to padding their messages with a lot of unnecessary words. When in doubt, apply the KISS principle: keep it short and simple.

Example

Wordy—107 words

Dear Eleanor,

It has come to my attention, that our esteemed client, Bill Hawkins, is celebrating a 15-year anniversary with our company. I believe that it would be appropriate and also a gesture of our company's goodwill and thanks for his loyalty through those years, if we offered him an invitation to our company's golf tournament. I would appreciate your letting me know, as soon as it is feasible, whether it will be possible or not to add Bill's name to the list for the tournament.

Once again, I appreciate your looking into this matter for me, and I look forward to hearing from you soon.

Regards,

Not So Wordy – 53 words

Dear Eleanor,

Bill Hawkins has been a great client for 15 years. To say thank-you for his loyalty, I'd like to invite him to our company golf tournament. Please let me know whether I can invite Bill. I'd like to let him know by Friday.

Thanks for looking into this for me.

Regards,

For a simple request such as the one above, there's no reason to be anything but brief and to the point. In both cases, we know that Bill is a valuable client, and in both cases, we know that the writer wants to invite him to the company golf tournament. And you can still use the magic words, please and thank you.

Below are some tips for eliminating wordiness in your writing. For more information, check:

http://leo.stcloudstate.edu/style/wordiness.html

http://www.grammarly.com/blog/2015/make-your-writing-clearer-6-tips-for-re-wording-sentencesa/

1. Eliminate Qualifiers

Sentences are rarely improved by the addition of words such as extremely, really, and very. Find a better adjective to replace phrases with those words in them or just leave them out entirely.

Extremely sad – sad, crushed, despondent, bereft, grief-stricken

Very happy – happy, cheerful, overjoyed, delirious, thrilled

Really hungry – hungry, starving, ravenous, famished

Very angry – angry, livid, furious, apoplectic …

2. Eliminate There is, Here is, There was, It was, It is, There will be, It will be

These words can usually be dropped from the beginnings of sentences.

There were ten people waiting in line ahead of me.
Ten people were ahead of me in line.

It was an informative meeting.
The meeting was informative.

There will be a meeting at noon tomorrow.
The meeting is at noon tomorrow.

3. Combine sentences that repeat the same information.

The meeting is a noon tomorrow. We will be meeting in the boardroom to discuss the new pension plan.
The meeting to discuss the new pension plan is at noon tomorrow in the boardroom.

I just spoke to Bill. He talked about the new system of keeping track of accounts. He said the new system would be faster to learn.
Bill said the new system of keeping track of accounts would be faster to learn.

4. Eliminate longer phrases and replace with shorter words.

I've included a few examples below, so you can see what I mean. To see a more comprehensive list check here:
http://writing.wisc.edu/Handbook/CCS_wordyphrases.html

In order to meet the deadline ….
To meet the deadline ….

In consideration of the fact that the weather will be cold in January ….

Because the weather will be cold in January ….

At this moment in time, it's important to remember….
Now, it's ….
Today ….

IN SHORT

- Eliminate flowery, too formal language
- Eliminate qualifiers.
- Eliminate Here is, There is, etc.
- Combine sentences that contain the same information
- Eliminate longer phrases and replace with shorter words.

CHAPTER 7

Rules for Bullet Lists

Lists are a very efficient way to present information in your email, but they need to have a very specific format. Use bullets when listing a series of items. Use numbers when listing a set of steps that have to be followed in order or to prioritize the list by ranking the information in order.

Rules for the Lead In

If the lead-in that precedes the list is a complete sentence, you end it with a colon.

Examples

The following are the four points I'd like you to consider:

Here are the 5 steps you need to follow:

Please answer the following questions:

The material required includes the following:

If the lead-in is not a complete sentence, that means that the material following the lead-in is completing the sentence; therefore, the lead-in has no punctuation after it.

Examples

The four steps require to complete this project are

It's important to remember that

I'd appreciate your input on

Rules for Punctuation

Here are a couple of examples that show how the rest of the list is punctuated.

Example 1

Please complete the following and return them to me by Friday:

- Status Form 1303
- Standard Release 12
- Personnel Questionnaire
- Tax Form C39.

Example 2

In order to be ready for the meeting, you will need to

- review the Benson contract,
- bring tax information relating to the Morris partnership, and
- review the Hendley incorporation documents.

Note that in the above example, the list is punctuated as if it were written out as one long sentence with commas after the items in the list. It would look like the following:

In order to be ready for the meeting, you will need to review the Benson contract, bring tax information relating to the Morris partnership, and review the Hendley incorporation documents.

Rules for the contents

All of the items in the list need to follow the same pattern. In Example 2, all of the items in the list are nouns/things. In Example 2, every point begins with a verb/action: review, bring, review.

Here's an example of a list in which the items don't follow the same pattern.

On Friday morning
- Bring your laptop
- Go to meeting room B
- You'll need a 2G memory stick.

In the above example, the first two items begin with verbs (bring, go) and the third item is a sentence starting with the pronoun, you. Since all the items in the list need to match, the third item also needs to start with a verb.

On Monday morning
- bring your laptop
- go to meeting room B
- bring an empty 2G memory stick.

Here are two more before and after examples. When you write your lists correctly, it's called parallel construction.

When winter comes, we love to
- ski
- make snowmen
- skate in the park
- making snow angels at Grandma's house.

When winter comes, we love to
- ski
- make snowmen
- skate in the park
- make snow angels at Grandma's house.

Here are some steps you need to complete in order to write a report:
- Brainstorm ideas
- Find research sources
- Draft an outline
- Writing the first draft comes next.

Here are some steps you need to complete in order to write a report:
- Brainstorm ideas
- Find research sources
- Draft an outline
- Write the first draft.

IN SHORT

- If the lead-in is a complete sentence, it is followed by a colon.
- The items in a list preceded by a colon begin with a capital letter. If they are single words or phrases, they need no end punctuation. If they are short sentences, each sentence needs a period at the end.
- If the lead-in is not a complete sentence, no punctuation is required.
- The items in a list following an incomplete sentence do not begin with a capital letter and are followed by commas with a period at the end—as if you were writing it out as one long sentence.
- All items in the list need to follow the same format—parallel construction

CHAPTER 8

If You Are Asking for Something

Request letters generally follow the same format. In the **first paragraph**, explain what you are requesting. Put yourself in the reader's shoes. Think about what *you* would need to know before you could say yes or no the request. Include as much of the relevant information as possible to make the recipient's decision easier.

In the example below, the key to getting a positive response is to make sure that you are very clear about what you are asking for. The writer here has given Barney enough information to make a decision. Barney knows the time, the purpose, and the duration of the event.

In the **second paragraph**, offer the recipient more information or background to the request.

In the **concluding paragraph**, make sure that the recipient knows where to get more information and how he or she should reply to the request. If there is a deadline, make sure that it is clear to the recipient, so that you have enough time to contact someone else if the first person says no.

Example

Hi Barney,

I have been looking for a speaker for our next managers' lunch meeting, and Helen suggested that you would be a good person to ask. The hour-long meeting is on February 9 at 12:30 in the Atlantic board room, and the focus of the meeting is *meeting goals*. Our speakers usually talk for about fifteen minutes, and another ten minutes is set aside for questions. Helen said that we could learn a lot from you and how you achieved your goal of walking 2013 kilometers in 2013 and 2014 kilometers in 2014.

I'm sure the managers would be very interested to learn how you approached such a big task and how you overcame any problems. Our meetings are informal and lunch is provided.

Please let me know by January 17, if you can speak to our group. If you have any questions, please call me at extension 459. I look forward to hearing from you.

Sincerely,

Heather

Heather Wright

Vice-President
555-123-4567 ext. 89
hwright@thecompany.com

IN SHORT

- Explain what you are asking for at the beginning.
- Give the reader all the details he or she needs to make a decision.
- Make sure that the reader has two ways to contact you with his or her response.

CHAPTER 9

Email Etiquette

Email is a challenging medium. You need to respond quickly, write well, and make sure that you and your business look good.

Here are some suggestions to help make sure that the last item on the above list is guaranteed.

Skip the sarcasm and humor

Email is the most misunderstood medium of communication. What gets in the way of email doing its job well is the lack of context that the reader has when decoding the message. What you might think is great sarcasm or a witty remark, your reader can find insulting or hurtful. It's best just to stick with the facts and remember to say please and thank you. Check the link below to learn more about email and miscommunication.

https://www.psychologytoday.com/blog/contemporary-psychoanalysis-in-action/201502/why-is-there-so-much-miscommunication-email-and

Why Is There So Much Miscommunication Via Email and Text? How we interpret electronic messages is shaped by our feelings

Post published by The Contemporary Psychoanalysis Group on Feb 15, 2015 in Contemporary Psychoanalysis in Action

Style and Form

Terse incomplete sentences with spelling errors do not send the message that you are busy or too important to worry about writing correctly. You wouldn't expect to receive a message in that format from a junior employee, so why would you set the example of bad writing for all to see.

Use email to model professional standards that you want your employees to emulate when they are writing to customers. Even if your boss writes messages like this, there is no need for you to copy him or her.

FULL CAPS

Skip using full caps in your emails. When words are in full caps it means they are being shouted. You wouldn't shout at clients and co-workers in real life (though, I know it could be tempting), so don't do it on paper.

IN SHORT

- Don't try to be funny or use sarcasm.
- Always use correct spelling, grammar, and punctuation.
- Full Caps shout at your reader—don't use them

CHAPTER 10

Bulk Mail Tricks and EOM

Bulk Mail

Bulk mail needs to be handled with care. If you are sending a notice about a new product to a group of your clients, use the BCC box to enter their email addresses and put only your address in the TO box.

When you put all of your clients' email addresses in the TO box, every person that receives your message can also see the names and addresses of your other clients. Some of your clients might not appreciate having their email addresses shared, and others might not want everyone else to know that they are your client, especially if they are also working with other people in the field.

When you put their addresses into the BCC box, they only see your address and theirs. You maintain their privacy and save the time of creating separate emails.

EOM – End of Message

Using EOM is a time saver for everyone.

When you want to thank someone quickly, write your thank-you message in the subject line and end with EOM. For example, if someone has sent you links to some important information, you could reply and change the subject line to *Thanks for the great information. EOM.* When the person sees EOM, he or she knows that they don't have to open the email to read the message. You've put the message in the subject line.

If you and many others are invited to an event, don't click reply all. Just reply and change the subject line to include your acceptance of the invitation. Looking forward to the meeting on the 22nd. EOM

IN SHORT

- Use BCC to hide the names of all the recipients in a bulk mailing.
- Use EOM to put your short message in the subject line and to save your reader's time.

Last Words

There is no magic bullet for success in your career, but you can bet that making a good impression through your written communication won't hurt and may just set you above the rest.

Good luck with meeting your business goals. One of my business goals is to sell more books. If you found this guide of value, please stop by your online bookseller and leave a review. I appreciate your time and your honest comments.

This book is not carved in stone either. If there are other issues about the topic that you think I should address, please drop me a line, and I can always add it to the next edition.

hwrightwriter@gmail.com

ABOUT THE AUTHOR

Heather Wright is a freelance writer and part-time college instructor teaching business communications. Heather worked for many years in companies, both local and global in scope, and now runs her own freelance writing business. Through these experiences, she developed her own communications skill set that she now shares in her Better Business Communications books and with her students in the classroom, as well as in the workplace.

Printed in Great Britain
by Amazon